VAGUS NERVE

THE COMPLETE GUIDE TO STIMULATING THE VAGUS NERVE, BALANCING STRESS, AND ENHANCING PHYSICAL AND MENTAL HEALTH

THERON VAYNE

CONTENTS

INTRODUCTION: YOUR HIDDEN ALLY FOR WELL-BEING

Welcome to a journey that could transform your life —or at the very least, offer you a new and surprising perspective full of potential. This book doesn't present an abstract concept or a distant theory, but rather a phenomenon that resides within you: a "hidden ally" capable of significantly enhancing your physical and mental well-being—the vagus nerve.

Yes, the vagus nerve. You may have heard of it, but do you truly know what it is and how it works? Don't worry if it feels unfamiliar right now. In this book, I will guide you step by step to uncover the workings of this extraordinary system that regulates numerous aspects of your body and mind. It's like unlocking a door to deeper, more enduring well-being—well-being that extends beyond the mere absence of illness and embraces a harmonious physical and emotional balance, enabling you to live each day to the fullest.

Vagus Nerve: A Fundamental Role in Our Well-Being

The vagus nerve is one of the most powerful and fascinating structures in the human body. It is the primary "cable" connecting the brain to vital organs such as the heart, lungs, stomach, intestines, and even the throat. Its name comes from the Latin word *vagus*, meaning "wandering," a fitting description for a nerve that extends through an intricate network across your body, influencing countless physiological and psychological functions.

You might not realize it, but the vagus nerve plays a critical role in the autonomic nervous system, which governs the body's involuntary functions like breathing, digestion, and heart rate. It's also pivotal to our ability to "slow down"—shifting from a heightened state (fight or flight) to a state of relaxation that fosters calm and recovery.

Here's the good news: the vagus nerve can be trained. By stimulating it, you can reduce stress, improve your mood, boost your energy, and strengthen both your physical and mental health. This isn't a random occurrence; it's a process you can actively influence using simple, effective techniques that you'll learn throughout this book.

How the Vagus Nerve Affects Our Body and Mind

Imagine feeling stressed, anxious, or overwhelmed by the demands of daily life. Your body responds by activating the sympathetic nervous system, triggering the fight-or-flight response: your heart races, your breathing becomes shallow and quick, and your muscles tense. Left unchecked, this constant state of activation can lead to physical and mental exhaustion.

Now, think of the vagus nerve as a control switch capable of turning off this state of hyper-alertness and guiding you back to calm and recovery. When the vagus nerve is stimulated, it activates the parasympathetic nervous system, resetting your body: your heart rate slows, your breathing deepens, and your muscles relax. This isn't just about "feeling better"—it's about tangible health improvements like reduced inflammation, lower blood pressure, and enhanced immune function.

Beyond the physical benefits, the vagus nerve has a profound impact on mental health. Neuroscience research reveals that proper vagus nerve stimulation can elevate your mood, bolster resilience against stress, and enhance emotional regulation. Simply put, stimulating the vagus nerve makes you stronger, calmer, and more balanced—physically and mentally.

The Goals of This Book

The objective of this book is simple: to equip you with the tools to use the vagus nerve as a powerful instrument for personal transformation. You'll discover natural methods to stimulate it through daily practices that help reduce stress, boost well-being, and optimize your health. You don't need to be an expert in neuroscience to grasp and apply the insights shared here. This book is written for every-one, regardless of your prior knowledge or experience.

The journey you are about to embark on will deepen your understanding of your body and mind. You'll learn how vagus nerve stimulation can become a safe, accessible, and highly effective prac-tice to enhance your daily life. The beauty of this process lies in its simplicity—each small step brings you closer to a more peaceful, energetic, and balanced version of yourself.

Discover the Transformative Power of the Vagus Nerve

The vagus nerve is a remarkable ally that can be activated daily through simple and natural practices. In this book, you will not only delve into its biological functions but also learn practical methods to activate and enhance its role. From conscious breathing and cold exposure to muscle relaxation and meditation, each chapter introduces effective strategies to integrate into your daily life.

Whether you aim to improve your mood, reduce stress, or find better ways to navigate daily challenges, stimulating the vagus nerve is a crucial step. Every exercise and every insight shared in this book will guide you toward a state of well-being that transcends the superficial, fostering holistic health that encompasses mind, body, and spirit.

Start your journey today. The vagus nerve is ready to support you in achieving profound and lasting well-being. With each step, you will uncover the keys to improving your health in natural and meaningful ways. Are you ready? Turn the page and discover everything the vagus nerve has to offer.

CHAPTER 1: WHAT IS THE VAGUS NERVE? BASIC ANATOMY AND FUNCTION

When we reflect on our bodies, we often overlook the intricate systems that operate silently and remarkably efficiently to keep us functioning. One of the most vital yet often unrecognized players in these processes—impacting nearly every facet of our physical and mental well-being—is the vagus nerve. Acting as a "communication superhighway," this nerve is crucial for maintaining the balance between our body and mind. But what exactly is the vagus nerve? How does it function? And how can we harness its potential to enhance our health?

In this chapter, we'll delve into its anatomy, role, and influence on numerous physiological and emotional processes. You'll discover how a nerve extending from the brainstem to the abdomen wields such a significant impact on our well-being and learn practical ways to stimulate it to promote health and inner peace.

The Anatomical Structure of the Vagus Nerve

The vagus nerve is one of the twelve cranial nerves, emerging directly from the brain and brainstem. Its name, derived from the Latin word *vagus*, meaning "wandering," aptly describes its extensive reach throughout the body, branching into numerous vital regions.

Originating in the brainstem, specifically from the vagus nerve nucleus located in the medulla oblongata, it extends to the heart, lungs, stomach, intestines, and even the throat. As the longest cranial nerve, it is integral to a variety of essential bodily functions.

Primarily associated with the parasympathetic nervous system—a division of the autonomic nervous system—the vagus nerve serves as a regulator of relaxation and recovery. In contrast to the sympathetic system, which activates the "fight or flight" response, the parasympathetic system, with the vagus nerve at its core, promotes calm and balance.

The Function of the Vagus Nerve in the Body

The vagus nerve serves as a vital "bridge," linking the brain to multiple key organs and facilitating a broad spectrum of physiological functions. Here's how it interacts with some of the body's major systems:

1. **Heart and Circulation:** The vagus nerve plays a pivotal role in regulating heart rate. When activated, it slows the heart rate, lowers blood pressure, and induces a state of relaxation. It acts as a "brake," helping the body transition from stress to balance.

2. **Lungs and Breathing:** This nerve also governs respiratory function, stimulating the reflex to expel air during exhalation. Its activation encourages deeper, slower breathing, a cornerstone of parasympathetic activation and stress reduction.

3. **Digestive System:** One of the most fascinating roles of the vagus nerve is in digestion. It stimulates gastric juice production, enhances intestinal peristalsis (the movement of food

through the intestines), and supports nutrient absorption, optimizing the digestive process.

4. **Immune System:** The vagus nerve significantly influences inflammation regulation. Stimulating the nerve can help reduce systemic inflammation, strengthening the immune response and mitigating the risk of chronic diseases.

5. **Throat and Voice:** The vagus nerve innervates the larynx, pharynx, and other structures critical for voice production and swallowing. Its stimulation has been linked to improved emotional expression and calmer, more effective communication.

Vagal Tone and Vagal Stimulation: Key Concepts

When discussing the vagus nerve, two terms frequently arise: "vagal tone" and "vagal stimulation." Understanding these concepts can unlock insights into its profound physiological impact.

- **Vagal Tone:** Vagal tone reflects the "strength" and responsiveness of the vagus nerve in meeting the body's needs.

High vagal tone indicates a healthy ability to transition from stress (driven by the sympathetic system) to relaxation (guided by the parasympathetic system). This is associated with better emotional resilience, stress management, and overall health.

- **Vagal Stimulation:** Stimulating the vagus nerve involves activating it through various techniques—such as deep breathing, cold exposure, or mindfulness exercises—to enhance its functionality and promote well-being.

Vagus Nerve Stimulation: Unlocking the Power of the Parasympathetic System

Stimulating the vagus nerve involves intentionally activating this critical component of the autonomic nervous system to enhance overall well-being. Various methods, including deep breathing exercises, mindfulness meditation, cold exposure techniques, and even electrical stimulation (used in medical therapies), can directly influence the parasympathetic system. These approaches help reduce stress, promote recovery, and support relaxation.

Innervation of the Vagus Nerve Across Major Organs

As we have discussed, the vagus nerve acts as a "highway" of communication between the brain and the body's vital systems. To truly appreciate its significance, it's important to understand its specific connections and functions. The vagus nerve innervates the following key organs:

- **Brain:** The vagus nerve plays a role in regulating emotional responses, mood, and the perception of pain by transmitting afferent and efferent signals.
- **Heart:** It helps regulate heart rate and blood pressure, functioning as a natural "brake" to promote calm and balance.
- **Lungs:** It supports breathing patterns, enhancing pulmonary ventilation and facilitating a relaxed respiratory rhythm.
- **Stomach and Intestines:** The vagus nerve is crucial for intestinal motility, digestion, and nutrient absorption, ensuring proper gastrointestinal function.
- **Liver:** It influences bile secretion and metabolic processes, contributing to efficient energy regulation.

- **Kidneys:** The vagus nerve also impacts renal function, assisting in maintaining the body's fluid and electrolyte balance.

The vagus nerve is one of the most intricate and vital structures in the human body. Its extensive anatomy and its role in modulating the autonomic nervous system make it a cornerstone of health. By understanding its functions and learning how to stimulate it, we can take significant steps towards improved health, reduced stress, and achieving physiological and emotional balance.

CHAPTER 2: THE VAGUS NERVE AND THE AUTONOMIC NERVOUS SYSTEM

Throughout our lives, our bodies constantly adapt and respond to both external and internal stimuli. To do this efficiently, without requiring us to consciously manage every action, our bodies rely on a sophisticated system of automatic regulation working behind the scenes. This system is the autonomic nervous system (ANS), and the vagus nerve, which we are focusing on, is one of its key components. But how exactly does it work? And why is it so crucial for managing stress and our overall well-being?

In this chapter, I will guide you through the autonomic nervous system, emphasizing the vital role of the vagus nerve in balancing two forces that regulate our state of health: the sympathetic and parasympathetic nervous systems. Together, we will explore how their interaction affects both our emotional and physical state, and how we can leverage this balance to improve our daily lives, reduce stress, and prevent anxiety.

The Autonomic Nervous System: Subconscious Regulation

The autonomic nervous system (ANS) is a network of nerves that regulates bodily functions which do not require conscious effort: from heart rate to digestion, from breathing to sweating. Its purpose is to maintain homeostasis, or the internal balance of the body, in response to changes in the environment, emotions, and behaviors.

The ANS is divided into two primary components:

1. **The Sympathetic System**: Responsible for preparing the body to face stressful or dangerous situations by activating the "fight or flight" response. It stimulates adrenaline production, increases heart rate, dilates the pupils, and temporarily slows down non-essential functions, such as digestion.

2. **The Parasympathetic System:** Often referred to as the "rest and digest" system, it performs the opposite function. When the body is in a state of relaxation, the parasympathetic system reduces heart rate, promotes digestion, and facilitates energy recovery.

The Vagus Nerve: The Protagonist of the Parasympathetic System

As we discussed in the previous chapter, the vagus nerve is the main nerve of the parasympathetic system. It extends from the brainstem to key organs such as the heart, lungs, stomach, and intestines. The vagus nerve sends signals that help the body "calm down" after a stress response. In essence, the vagus nerve is our ally in recovery, helping restore balance after periods of stress or exertion.

Imagine being in a stressful situation. The sympathetic system activates: your heart races, your mind fills with rapid thoughts, and your muscles tense up. This is where the vagus nerve comes into play, helping to bring the body back to a state of calm. By stimulating the vagus nerve, we can slow the heart rate, lower blood pressure, reduce muscle tension, and promote deeper, slower breathing. These effects are critical in preventing stress from becoming chronic and safeguarding the body from long-term harm.

Sympathetic and Parasympathetic Balance

The autonomic nervous system is not made up of two separate forces; instead, the sympathetic and parasympathetic systems are in constant dialogue, striving to maintain dynamic balance. When the sympathetic system takes over, we may feel over-whelmed by stress, anxiety, and difficulty relaxing. Conversely, when the parasympathetic system dominates, we feel calmer, more centered, and better equipped to face daily challenges with greater serenity.

However, our modern lifestyle—characterized by hectic schedules, pressures, and constant stimulation—often triggers persistent sympathetic activation. This state of "over-activation" is frequently linked to symptoms such as anxiety, fatigue, and sleep disturbances. This is where our ability to stimulate the vagus nerve becomes essential, promoting a reversal of this pattern and allowing the body to return to a balanced state.

How the Vagus Nerve Affects Stress Management

Chronic stress is one of the primary factors that threaten both our mental and physical health. When we are stressed, the body becomes vulnerable to cardiovascular diseases, diabetes, gastrointestinal issues, and anxiety. Vagus nerve stimulation is one of the most effective techniques for counteracting these adverse effects.

The Vagus Nerve and Stress Management

The vagus nerve has the power to reduce the release of stress hormones, such as cortisol, promoting relaxation and recovery. Effective vagal stimulation helps reduce sympathetic activation, decreasing feelings of being overwhelmed by external stimuli. This is why learning how to properly stimulate the vagus nerve is essential not only for our physical health, but also for our emotional and psychological well-being.

The Vagus Nerve and Its Role in Anxiety

One of the most fascinating aspects of vagus nerve stimulation is its potential for treating anxiety. People who suffer from anxiety tend to live in a state of constant sympathetic activation, with the body "sensing" threats even when none exist. Vagus nerve stimulation helps break this cycle, bringing the body back into a state of relaxation and reducing anxiety levels.

Recent studies have shown that vagus nerve stimulation can significantly reduce anxiety symptoms, improve psychological resilience, and promote emotional stability. But how can you practically stimulate the vagus nerve?

Vagus Nerve Stimulation to Reduce Stress and Anxiety

There are several ways to stimulate the vagus nerve and help balance the sympathetic and parasympathetic nervous systems. Many of these methods can be easily integrated into your daily routine, offering tangible support for stress management. Some examples include:

1. **Deep, mindful breathing:**
   Diaphragmatic breathing directly stimulates the vagus nerve, helping to slow the heart rate and promote relaxation.

2. **Meditation and mindfulness:**
   Meditation focused on the breath
   increases vagus nerve activity and
   improves emotional regulation.
3. **Cold exposure techniques:** Cold baths,
   cold showers, or even brief exposure to
   cold temperatures stimulate the vagus
   nerve, promoting stress recovery.
4. **Yoga and relaxation techniques:** Yoga
   poses, especially those that encourage
   deep breathing, are excellent for
   stimulating the vagus nerve.
5. **Singing and laughter:** Yes, even
   pleasurable activities like singing or
   laughing stimulate the vagus nerve and
   improve vagal tone.

The vagus nerve is a powerful ally in managing stress and anxiety. Learning to effectively activate it can help restore balance to both body and mind, enhancing long-term well-being. The key is understanding its fundamental role within the autonomic nervous system and applying techniques that promote its activation.

CHAPTER 3: THE VAGUS NERVE AND THE BRAIN: MIND AND BODY CONNECTED

In the scientific world, we tend to think of the mind and body as separate entities. However, the vagus nerve reveals that the mind and body are deeply connected, united by a network of invisible communications that orchestrate our experience of well-being. In this chapter, we will explore how the vagus nerve plays a fundamental role in mental health, influencing our mood, emotions, and brain state. Understanding this connection will give you the tools to improve your daily life, reduce stress, and promote long-term mental balance.

The Vagus Nerve and the Limbic System: The Center of Emotions

To fully understand how the vagus nerve affects

mental health, we must first explore a fundamental part of our brain: the limbic system. This system is our "emotional center" and includes key structures such as the amygdala, hippocampus, and thalamus. It is where emotions arise, but it is also where behavioral responses to emotional experiences are formed.

The vagus nerve plays a crucial role in regulating the activity of this "emotional hub." When we stimulate the vagus nerve, we send a calming signal to the amygdala, reducing our automatic emotional response. The amygdala, which typically reacts to threatening or stressful stimuli with fear and anxiety, becomes more receptive when the vagus nerve is active, facilitating a more balanced and less reactive stress response.

This process is essential for emotional regulation. Stimulating the vagus nerve helps promote mental calm, reduce anxiety, and improve our emotional resilience. In fact, vagal activation helps the brain reorient itself, bringing balance to emotional reactions and creating a state of inner serenity.

Neurotransmitters and the Link Between the Vagus Nerve and the Brain

In addition to modulating the activity of the limbic system, the vagus nerve interacts directly with several neurotransmitters that regulate our mood and behavior. These include serotonin, GABA (gamma-aminobutyric acid), and dopamine. All of these neurotransmitters are involved in regulating mood, motivation, and the response to stress.

- **Serotonin:** Often called the "happy neurotransmitter," serotonin plays a crucial role in our psychological well-being. It is responsible for regulating mood, sleep, and appetite. The vagus nerve stimulates the production and release of serotonin, which improves our mood and helps reduce feelings of sadness or anxiety.
- **GABA:** This neurotransmitter is a powerful brain calmer, reducing neuronal activity and promoting relaxation. The vagus nerve increases the production of GABA, promoting a sense of calm and helping reduce the mental

agitation that often accompanies stress or anxiety.

- **Dopamine**: Dopamine is linked to the brain's reward system, influencing motivation, gratification, and concentration. Proper vagus nerve activation can support a balanced production of dopamine, helping to improve motivation and cognitive energy without the need for external stimulants.

Vagus Nerve Stimulation: A Powerful Tool Against Stress

The connection between the vagus nerve and mental health is particularly visible in the way the vagus nerve counterbalances the effects of stress. When we are under stress, the sympathetic nervous system activates, preparing the body for an acute fight-or-flight response. This response is useful in emergency situations, but when our body remains in a state of high activation for too long, it can lead to negative effects on both mental and physical health.

The vagus nerve, as part of the parasympathetic nervous system, acts as an antidote to this hyperactive state. By stimulating the vagus nerve, we promote a "rest-and-digest" response, which counterbalances the sympathetic nervous system's effect. This leads to a reduction in heart rate, blood pressure, and levels of the stress hormone cortisol. This not only helps improve our physical health, but also has a direct impact on our mental state, reducing symptoms of anxiety, irritability, and worry.

The Feedback Loop: Mind and Body

One of the most fascinating features of the vagus nerve is the feedback loop it creates between the brain and the body. As the vagus nerve transmits calming signals from the body to the brain, the brain responds by regulating the activity of the autonomic nervous system. This feedback loop helps maintain balance between emotions and physical states, creating a self-regulating system that promotes well-being.

When we stimulate the vagus nerve, for example through deep breathing exercises or meditation practices, we send a calming signal to the brain. This, in turn, reduces the activity of the amygdala and lowers stress levels. The mind, in turn, responds by reducing worry and enhancing a sense of well-being. In this way, the vagus nerve acts as a bridge between the mind and the body, creating a connection that improves our overall experience of health.

Understanding the role of the vagus nerve in brain function is a critical step in understanding how the mind and body are inseparable. Stimulating the vagus nerve not only helps regulate our stress response, but also improves our ability to manage complex emotions, promoting lasting psychological balance. The connection between the vagus nerve and mental health is an essential aspect of our ability to live more peacefully and consciously, and through simple stimulation techniques, we can utilize this untapped potential to improve our quality of life.

CHAPTER 4: THE VAGUS NERVE AND PHYSICAL HEALTH

When we think about our bodies, we often focus on the actions we perform consciously: moving our muscles, breathing, or walking. But behind every movement, every heartbeat, every breath, there are invisible processes that operate without our full awareness. The autonomic nervous system, of which the vagus nerve is a fundamental component, regulates many of these invisible functions, influencing our physical health in ways that are continually being investigated by science.

In this chapter, we explore how the vagus nerve contributes to our physical health, intervening in several key systems of our body, from digestion to heart rate, regulating inflammation and supporting immunity. Discovering how to stimulate and optimize vagal activity can not only improve your overall well-being, but also help you feel more in tune with your body, as if you are giving the right boost to its natural processes to restore health and vitality.

The Vagus Nerve and Digestion: A Natural Healing Process

The first, and perhaps most obvious, impact the vagus nerve has on physical health concerns the digestive process. As many know, digestion is not just a matter of breaking down food into smaller molecules, but involves a series of complex functions that require careful coordination between various systems: muscular, enzymatic, hormonal, and nervous.

The vagus nerve plays a central role in this coordination. It is the main player in the parasympathetic nervous system, which allows our body to "recover" after the activation of the sympathetic nervous system, the "fight or flight" response that sends us into stress mode. When the vagus nerve is active, it signals the body to "slow down" and focus on digestive and restorative functions, such as digestion and bowel care.

Stimulation of the vagus nerve helps improve bowel movement, promotes the production of digestive enzymes, and regulates nutrient absorption.

Furthermore, when we stimulate the vagus nerve, excess stomach acid production is reduced, preventing heartburn and improving digestive comfort. It is as if the body receives a signal to enter a more relaxed state, promoting an intestinal environment that optimizes digestion.

The Vagus Nerve and Immunity: A Protected Body

Another crucial aspect of the vagus nerve concerns the regulation of the immune system. In a world where we are constantly exposed to potential microbial and environmental threats, having a strong and well-balanced immune system is essential. The vagus nerve, through its involvement in the inflammatory response, has the power to modulate the activity of the immune system, keeping it in an optimal state.

Many studies have shown that the vagus nerve can reduce systemic inflammation. When the body is subjected to stress or an infection, the immune system responds by releasing a series of inflammatory molecules. However, too much inflammation is harmful to the body, increasing the risk of chronic diseases such as atherosclerosis, diabetes, and autoimmune diseases. The vagus nerve, however, can inhibit this process, signaling the body to reduce the production of inflammatory cytokines. In other words, by stimulating the vagus nerve, we can promote a balanced immune response, which protects us without triggering harmful inflammatory reactions.

Vagal stimulation has also been shown to be particularly useful in cases of chronic inflammatory diseases, such as rheumatoid arthritis and inflammatory bowel disease (IBD). With the vagus nerve acting as a brake on inflammation, the body is able to maintain a healthy balance, reducing the risks associated with an overactive immune system.

The Vagus Nerve and Heart Rate: A Relaxed Heart

Heart rate is another aspect that depends on the vagus nerve. When the vagus nerve is stimulated, the heart slows down, while when the sympathetic nervous system is active, the heart speeds up. In other words, the vagus nerve regulates the heart's response, ensuring that the heart doesn't work too hard when it doesn't need to. Vagal control over heart rate is essential to keeping our hearts healthy. A heart that beats too fast in response to chronic stress can increase the risk of cardiovascular disease. In contrast, stimulation of the vagus nerve helps slow the heart rate, reducing stress and promoting a state of calm. The balance between the sympathetic and parasympathetic nervous systems (in which the vagus nerve plays a key role) is essential for the proper functioning of our hearts.

Heart Rate Variability (HRV): A Key Indicator of Health

Heart rate variability (HRV) is an important indicator of health and well-being. High HRV signals a healthy autonomic nervous system that can quickly adjust to stress and bounce back faster. Stimulating the vagus nerve is one way to improve this variability, promoting a heart that can effectively handle daily challenges without compromising health.

The Vagus Nerve: A Powerful Ally in Reducing Inflammation

Inflammation is a natural response of the body to injury or infection. However, chronic inflammation can have devastating effects, contributing to diseases such as diabetes, heart disease, and cancer. The vagus nerve is crucial for regulating inflammation. With its ability to modulate inflammatory responses, the vagus nerve helps prevent the damage caused by persistent inflammation.

Research suggests that adequate stimulation of the vagus nerve can reduce levels of systemic inflammation, helping to maintain the body in optimal health. In practice, this means that you can not only handle stressful situations better but also help your body recover faster, preventing diseases linked to chronic inflammation.

As we have seen, the vagus nerve plays a central role in regulating numerous vital physical processes, including digestion, heart rate, immune response, and inflammation. Understanding how to stimulate the vagus nerve and optimize its functioning is key to maintaining a healthy body and promoting lasting balance between mind and body.
Every time we stimulate the vagus nerve, we are sending a signal to our body to relax, recover, and restore balance. It is an invitation to align with our natural biological rhythms, reducing stress and enhancing our overall quality of life. Whether it's through deep breathing, meditation, or other vagus nerve stimulation techniques, the vagus nerve is our invisible ally, ready to help us achieve optimal physical health.

CHAPTER 5: STIMULATING THE VAGUS NERVE: CONSCIOUS BREATHING

Imagine for a moment that you're experiencing a particularly stressful day. Deadlines are mounting, your thoughts are racing, and your body begins to respond to this internal pressure with growing anxiety. Your heart rate increases, your mind becomes cluttered, and your breathing becomes shallow and rapid. In these moments, we often find ourselves trapped in a vicious cycle of tension and stress, but there is a resource we can always rely on to help break this cycle: the vagus nerve.

The vagus nerve, one of the main structures of our autonomic nervous system, has the power to slow down our response to stress, bringing us back to a state of calm. But how can we activate it effectively, using it as a true "switch" that restores our balance?

The answer is conscious breathing. In this chapter, we will explore together how deep breathing techniques can stimulate the vagus nerve and how, through conscious breathing, we can improve our physical and mental well-being. The techniques you will learn in this chapter are not just theoretical exercises but practical tools that you can integrate into your daily life to better face challenges and achieve greater tranquility.

The Vagus Nerve and Breathing: A Deep Connection

Our autonomic nervous system, of which the vagus nerve is one of the main components, regulates many vital functions that occur without our conscious intervention: the heartbeat, digestion, blood pressure, and breathing itself. In particular, the vagus nerve regulates "vagal tone," which is our body's ability to slow down, recover, and manage stress. When vagal tone is high, our body is able to face challenges with greater resilience, recovering more quickly from stressful situations.

Conscious breathing is one of the most effective ways to activate the vagus nerve. Every deep, controlled breath sends a signal to the brain that stimulates the vagus nerve, triggering a calming response throughout the body. We can think of breathing as a "bridge" between the mind and the body: while the mind may be agitated and frenetic, the breath acts as an anchor, bringing everything back to calm. When we practice deep breathing techniques, we stimulate the part of the nervous system responsible for relaxation, slowing our heart rate, lowering blood pressure, and improving digestion.

Breathing Techniques for Vagus Nerve Stimulation

There are different breathing techniques that can be used to stimulate the vagus nerve. Each of them acts specifically on our body and mind, helping us slow down and promote a feeling of well-being. Let's explore the most effective ones.

1. Diaphragmatic (or Abdominal) Breathing

Diaphragmatic breathing is one of the most effective techniques for stimulating the vagus nerve. This type of breathing engages the diaphragm, the muscle that separates the chest from the abdomen, allowing the lungs to fill with air more deeply and efficiently.

How to do it:

- Sit in a quiet place with your back straight and relaxed.
- Place one hand on your chest and the other on your abdomen.
- Begin to inhale slowly and deeply through your nose, expanding your belly while keeping your chest as still as possible.
- Exhale slowly through your mouth, trying to empty your lungs completely while pulling your abdomen in.
- Continue breathing this way for a few minutes, focusing on the movement of your abdomen.

This technique helps reduce tension, stimulates the vagus nerve, and can significantly improve your ability to relax during stressful times.

2. 4-7-8 Breathing

The 4-7-8 breathing technique is another powerful method that stimulates the vagus nerve and promotes deep relaxation. It is especially useful when you need to calm down quickly or fall asleep.

How to do it:

- Begin by exhaling completely through your mouth.
- Inhale through your nose for a count of four seconds.
- Hold your breath for seven seconds.
- Exhale slowly through your mouth for a count of eight seconds, making a hissing sound.
- Repeat the cycle 4-5 times.

This technique helps reduce anxiety and promotes an immediate feeling of calm by stimulating the vagus nerve and lowering your heart rate.

3. Alternate Breathing (Nadi Shodhana)

Alternate breathing, or Nadi Shodhana, is a technique used in yoga that balances the autonomic nervous system and promotes mental calm. It stimulates the vagus nerve by encouraging the alternation of airflow through both nostrils, thus promoting relaxation and reducing stress.

How to do it:

- Sit in a comfortable and relaxed position.
- Use your right thumb to close your right nostril.
- Inhale slowly and deeply through your left nostril.
- Close the left nostril with your right ring finger and hold the breath for a moment.
- Open your right nostril and exhale slowly through it.
- Inhale slowly through your right nostril.
- Close the right nostril with your thumb and hold your breath again.
- Open the left nostril and exhale slowly through it.
- Continue alternating between the nostrils for a few minutes.

This practice balances the sympathetic and parasympathetic nervous systems, promoting a state of relaxation, reducing stress, and enhancing focus and concentration.

How to Incorporate Mindful Breathing into Your Daily Life

Now that you are familiar with the breathing techniques that stimulate the vagus nerve, it's time to integrate them into your daily routine. The beauty of mindful breathing is that it doesn't require special equipment or a lot of time, making it easy to practice anywhere: at home, at work, while traveling, or before bed.

Here are some tips for incorporating mindful breathing into your daily life:

1. **Start with short sessions:** Spend 3-5 minutes a day practicing deep breathing. You can begin each morning when you wake up or before going to bed.

2. **Use mindful breathing during stressful moments:** Whenever you feel overwhelmed, try a quick session of deep breathing. It's also helpful before facing situations that make you anxious or worried.

3. **Practice breathing during physical activity:** If you engage in sports or exercise, incorporate mindful breathing

to enhance recovery and reduce muscle tension.

Breath is a powerful resource we often take for granted. Yet, its potential to influence our physical and mental state is immense. By practicing mindful breathing, we can activate the vagus nerve and enter a state of deep calm, improving both our physical and mental well-being.

Start exploring the power of your breath today. Every breath you take is an opportunity to activate your vagus nerve, calm your mind, and restore balance to your body. Never underestimate the importance of mindful breathing. It's a simple yet powerful practice that will accompany you throughout your life, helping you feel more serene, focused, and in harmony with yourself.

CHAPTER 6: STIMULATING THE VAGUS NERVE: THE POWER OF COLD

Imagine stepping into a cold shower. The sensation of ice-cold water hitting your skin is intense, almost shocking, and for a moment, your body enters a state of alert. Your heart rate increases, your breathing deepens, your muscles tense. Despite the discomfort, there is something surprisingly liberating about it. Once the experience ends, you're left with a sense of energy, mental clarity, and inner calm that seems to have been activated by the cold itself.

This physical response to cold is not just an immediate reaction, but also a powerful tool for stimulating the vagus nerve, a key component of our autonomic nervous system. The vagus nerve plays a crucial role in our mental and physical well-being, helping us manage stress, reduce inflammation, and maintain balance among the various systems of the body.

In this chapter, we'll explore how cold exposure, through practices like cold showers and ice baths, activates the vagus nerve and offers numerous benefits for both mental and physical health. We'll also discover how these techniques, when practiced with awareness, can become a powerful resource for improving our general well-being, stimulating the mind, and promoting psychological resilience.

Cold as a Stimulus for Stimulating the Vagus Nerve

The vagus nerve is one of the primary pathways by which the parasympathetic nervous system, responsible for relaxation and stress management, communicates with the body. It's involved in many vital functions, such as controlling the heartbeat, digestion, and inflammatory responses. When vagal tone is high, the body can quickly recover from stress, heal faster, and maintain optimal health.

Exposure to cold directly stimulates the vagus nerve, triggering its calming effect. Although cold exposure may initially feel stressful, it acts as a "workout" for the body, enhancing resilience and improving the ability to cope with both physical and mental discomfort.

When we immerse ourselves in cold water or expose ourselves to cold temperatures, the body triggers several physiological responses, including vasoconstriction, which reduces blood flow to the skin in order to protect vital organs. This, in turn, activates the vagus nerve, helping restore balance to the nervous system and reduce the stress response. After exposure, as the body warms up, the vagus nerve helps calm the body, promoting the release of endorphins and dopamine—neurotransmitters that enhance feelings of well-being.

Vagus Nerve Stimulation Techniques Using Cold

There are various techniques that utilize cold to stimulate the vagus nerve. Some are easy to practice, while others require more effort, yet all offer significant benefits for both physical and mental health.

1. Cold Showers

Cold showers are probably the easiest and most immediate way to stimulate the vagus nerve. You don't have to immerse yourself completely in cold water, but even a short, controlled exposure can be extremely beneficial.

How to do it:

- Start with a warm shower, as you normally do, to relax your muscles and prepare your body.
- When you're ready, gradually lower the water temperature until it's cold, but not freezing (you can start with cool water and slowly increase the duration and intensity).
- Stay under the cold water for about 30 seconds, trying to stay calm and focus on your breathing.
- Exhale deeply, trying to slow your heart rate and promote relaxation.
- You can repeat the process once or twice, gradually increasing the time under the cold stream.

Cold showers help improve blood circulation, stimulate metabolism, strengthen the immune system, and enhance stress tolerance.

2. Ice Baths

Another powerful technique is the ice bath, which involves complete immersion in cold water (usually around 5-10°C) with the addition of ice. This method is used by extreme athletes and professional sportspeople to reduce muscle pain and speed up recovery, but it also offers extraordinary benefits for mental health and vagus nerve stimulation.

How to do it:

- Fill a tub with cold water and add ice until the temperature reaches between 5 and 10 degrees Celsius.
- Gently sit in the tub and gradually lower yourself, being careful not to subject your body to too much cold all at once.
- Keep your breathing slow and deep, focusing on staying calm as you adjust to the cold. Focus on the experience and the release of tension.
- Start with 2-3 minute exposures and gradually increase the duration as you get used to this practice.

Ice baths are powerful stimulants for the vagus

nerve, helping to reduce inflammation and increase vagal tone, which improves your long-term stress response.

3. Outdoor Cold Exposure

Although less common, cold exposure outdoors is another effective way to stimulate the vagus nerve. Practices such as walking in cold weather, or even exposure to cold air, can activate the parasympathetic nervous system, improving our resilience to stress.

How to do it:

- Go outside on a cold day, preferably when the temperature is moderately cold but not dangerous (10-15°C is ideal to start with).
- You can walk slowly, focusing on your breathing and the sensations in your body as you adjust to the cold.
- Breathe deeply and try to stay calm while the cold stimulates the vagus nerve.

This exposure to cold also helps improve your

mood, reducing anxiety and depression, and can have similar stress-reducing effects as meditation.

Mental and Physical Health Benefits

The benefits of cold exposure are not limited to vagus nerve stimulation. This practice also offers impressive effects on both mental and physical health. Some of the main benefits include:

- **Stress Reduction:** When approached consciously, cold exposure can help reduce cortisol levels, improving your ability to relax.
- **Increased Energy:** After exposure to cold, the body releases endorphins, boosting energy and improving mood.
- **Immune System Boost:** Exposure to cold stimulates the immune system, increasing the production of white blood cells and enhancing the inflammatory response.
- **Increased Psychological Resilience:** Consciously confronting cold improves our ability to resist psychological stress, conditioning the body and mind to stay calm in the face of challenges.

Cold exposure is not just a physical challenge but a great way to stimulate the vagus nerve and enhance our well-being. Through practices like cold showers, ice baths, and cold exposure outdoors, we can activate our parasympathetic system, reduce stress, and foster a sense of calm and vitality.

If you've never tried cold as a tool for well-being, I encourage you to start gradually and carefully. Each small exposure will help you rediscover your resilience, inner strength, and the power to improve your mind-body balance.

CHAPTER 7: STIMULATING THE VAGUS NERVE: SOUNDS AND VIBRATIONS

Imagine being immersed in a tranquil atmosphere, where every sound seems to envelop you in a deep sense of calm. Perhaps you are listening to the gentle tones of a Tibetan singing bowl, or the deep, resonant rhythm of meditative music. In this state, your breathing becomes slower and deeper, your heartbeat regular, and a feeling of calmness surrounds you. What you are experiencing, even if it may seem like a simple musical experience, is actually a powerful stimulation of the vagus nerve, the heart of our parasympathetic nervous system.

The vagus nerve is responsible for many vital functions, including controlling the heartbeat, digestion, and regulating stress. When vagal tone is high, the body is better able to achieve a state of relaxation, reduce inflammation, and improve overall well-being. One of the most fascinating and effective ways to stimulate the vagus nerve is through sounds and vibrations. Techniques such as singing, humming (producing resonating sounds with your voice), and listening to music or specific frequencies are natural and profoundly effective tools for strengthening our nervous system and promoting relaxation.

In this chapter, we will explore the connection between sound, vibration, and the vagus nerve, discovering how these practices can become extraordinary allies in managing stress, improving mood, and enhancing both physical and mental health. I will also guide you through some practical exercises, which you can easily integrate into your daily routine, to maximize the power of these techniques.

The Connection Between Sound, Vibration, and the Vagus Nerve

Sound and vibration are, in fact, two of the most powerful stimuli that influence our body at a neuro-logical level. Every sound we perceive generates vibrations that, through the ear, reach the brain, influencing our emotional state, breathing, and even our physiology. The perception of sounds is closely linked to the autonomic nervous system, which regulates many of the automatic functions of the body, such as heartbeat, breathing, and digestion.

The vagus nerve, in particular, responds to sound and vibration stimuli. Vibration, in fact, is able to affect the frequency of brain waves, directly influencing our response to stress. When our nervous system perceives sounds and vibrations that promote a sense of tranquility, it activates the vagus nerve to encourage a decrease in heart rate, deeper breathing, and muscle relaxation.

Even if we are not always aware of it, the response to sound is immediate and profound. When we listen to relaxing music or participate in an activity that involves our body in vibration, such as singing or humming, our parasympathetic nervous system is activated, helping to reduce levels of cortisol (the stress hormone) and improve our emotional and physical well-being.

How Sounds and Vibrations Stimulate the Vagus Nerve

Sound vibrations, especially those emitted by our voice, are among the most direct and effective forms of stimulation for the vagus nerve. There are different types of sounds that can have various effects on our body, and understanding how to use them is essential to strengthen our nervous system.

1. Singing

Singing is one of the oldest and most powerful forms of vagus nerve stimulation. When we sing, our voice produces vibrations that travel through our body, directly reaching the vagus nerve, especially in the throat area, where this nerve has one of its most sensitive endings. Singing also promotes deep breathing, which is crucial for stimulating the vagus nerve and bringing the body into a state of relaxation.

How to do it:

- Choose a song that you enjoy and that makes you feel good. Don't worry about the perfection of the sound: the important thing is to sing from the heart and focus on the vibrations you feel in your body.
- While singing, try to feel the vibrations in specific points such as the head, chest, and throat. This will help you stimulate the vagus nerve naturally.

- If you want to intensify the effect, sing softly, focusing on the sensation of resonance, or try humming, a technique that stimulates the vagus nerve even more.

2. Humming

Humming is a practice that uses the sound vibrations emitted by our voice, but with an added feature: when we hum, the vibrations are amplified in the nasal cavity and head, creating a particularly beneficial stimulation for the vagus nerve. Humming not only promotes deep relaxation but can also be a powerful way to calm and focus ourselves.

How to do it:

- Sit in a quiet place and close your eyes.
- Start making a deep, steady hum with your mouth closed, as if you were humming a melody.
- Feel the vibrations resonating through your body, especially in the head and chest area.

- Breathe slowly and deeply as you continue humming, trying to stay focused on the sound and the sensations you feel.

3. Listening to Music

Music is another effective tool for stimulating the vagus nerve. Relaxing melodies, binaural beats, and nature sounds can reduce tension, improve sleep quality, and decrease stress. Different types of music interact directly with our autonomic nervous system, helping to regulate heart rate and breathing.

How to do it:

- Listen to music that helps you relax. The music can include classical pieces, nature sounds, or binaural beats. The key is to choose something that helps clear your mind and focus on the present.
- Find a quiet spot and sit or lie down in a comfortable position. Let the sounds wash over you and focus on the sensations each note evokes in your body.
- If possible, listen to the music with headphones that help you fully immerse yourself in the sound.

4. Binaural Frequencies

Binaural frequencies are a type of sound created when two slightly different tones are played in each ear. These tones interact in the brain, which perceives them as a third tone, and can influence our mental state, promoting relaxation or concentration. Binaural frequencies are especially effective at stimulating the vagus nerve, enhancing sleep quality, and aiding in stress management.

How to do it:

- Find an audio track with binaural frequencies specifically designed for relaxation or well-being.
- Use headphones for a better perception of the sound and sit in a quiet place, closing your eyes.
- Let the frequencies wash over you and allow your body to fully relax.

Practical Exercises for Stimulating the Vagus Nerve with Sound

To integrate these concepts into your daily routine, here are some practical exercises you can try whenever you need to reduce stress and stimulate your vagus nerve:

1. **Intentional Humming:** Every morning, dedicate five minutes to humming. Sit comfortably, close your eyes, and begin humming slowly. Focus on the vibrations in your body and aim to slow down your breathing while making the sound.

2. **Relaxing Music Moment:** Every evening, before going to sleep, listen to a song that makes you feel good, with a slow and relaxing rhythm. Focus on the music and let its sound fill your body, calming your nervous system.

3. **Meditation with Binaural Frequencies:** Try meditating with specific binaural frequencies designed for relaxation or sleep improvement. Dedicate at least 10 minutes a day to listening to these sounds, helping your body and mind release all tension.

The power of sound and vibration to stimulate the vagus nerve is remarkable. These exercises will not only help reduce stress but can also improve your ability to concentrate, promote quality sleep, and enhance your mental and physical health. By incorporating these practices into your daily life, you'll gain a significant advantage in enhancing your mental and physical balance, helping you feel calmer, more centered, and more in harmony with yourself.

CHAPTER 8: THE VAGUS NERVE AND MUSCLE RELAXATION

Your body is relaxed, your muscles are no longer tense, and your breathing flows gently. In this state, you activate the power of your vagus nerve, an invisible but powerful ally that regulates your physical and mental well-being. When we stimulate this nerve, we trigger a relaxation response that involves the entire body, reducing stress and promoting a sense of tranquility.

This chapter will explore how muscle relaxation can positively impact vagal tone, and how integrating relaxation techniques into your daily routine can significantly improve your health. The vagus nerve is a key component of our parasympathetic nervous system, responsible for initiating the relaxation response in the body after a period of stress. It helps slow down the heart rate, deepens the breathing, and relaxes the muscles. When vagal tone is high, our body is better equipped to respond to stress efficiently, recovering quickly from exertion and restoring balance. This mechanism is essential for coping with daily challenges without overwhelming or harming the body.

But how can we effectively stimulate the vagus nerve to promote muscle relaxation? How can we train our body to enter a state of deep and lasting calm? Together, we will explore the most effective techniques—from progressive relaxation to yoga—that can help us train our body to respond better to stress and improve our vagal tone.

Progressive Muscle Relaxation: An Art That Restores Balance

Progressive muscle relaxation (PMR) is a scientifically proven technique that involves systematically relaxing specific muscle groups, one at a time. The principle behind this technique is that, through the tension and subsequent relaxation of muscles, we can teach our body to recognize the difference between tension and relaxation, promoting a reduction in stress levels and improving vagal tone.

In practice, PMR leads you through a process of body awareness, where each part of your body is examined, first in a state of tension, then in a state of relaxation. This process helps focus your attention on the body and release accumulated tension. Over time, the body becomes more sensitive to muscle tension and better able to release it, leading to a state of relaxation that stimulates the vagus nerve and promotes a sense of calm.

How to: Progressive Muscle Relaxation Exercise

1. **Preparation:** Sit or lie down in a quiet place where you will not be disturbed. Make sure you have time and privacy to fully focus on yourself.
2. **Start with your feet:** Bring your attention to your feet. Flex your feet toward you, squeeze your toes, and hold the tension for about 5-10 seconds. Then, slowly release the tension, focusing on the sensation of relaxation that follows.
3. **Work your way up:** Move to your calves, thighs, abdomen, chest, arms, face, and finally your head. In each area, tighten the muscles for a few seconds and then release completely. You will feel the difference between tension and relaxation in every part of your body.

4. **Mindful Breathing:** During the exercise, pay attention to your breathing. Inhale deeply as you tighten the muscles, and exhale slowly as you relax them. This will help synchronize the muscle relaxation with the activation of the vagus nerve.

Yoga: The Movement That Relaxes and Awakens the Vagus Nerve

Yoga is another very powerful technique to stimulate the vagus nerve and promote muscle relaxation. Yoga poses (or asanas) are designed to release tension from the body, improve posture, and encourage deep breathing, which in turn stimulates the vagus nerve. The combination of slow movement and mindful breathing is a true therapeutic tool for both body and mind.

Yoga stimulates the vagus nerve through two main mechanisms: the first is deep breathing. During a yoga practice, breathing is a fundamental element. By inhaling and exhaling in a deep and controlled way, the parasympathetic system is activated, lowering the heart rate and relaxing the muscles. The second mechanism is movement. Each yoga pose is designed to lengthen the muscles, improve flexibility, reduce stiffness, and promote comprehensive relaxation of the body.

Yoga to Stimulate the Vagus Nerve

1. **Deep Breathing (Pranayama):** One of the most effective breathing techniques in yoga is ujjayi breathing, which involves inhaling and exhaling through the nose while creating a soft, ocean-like sound. This type of breathing calms the mind and stimulates the vagus nerve, improving stress management.

2. **Child's Pose (Balasana):** In this pose, you kneel with your forehead resting on the mat and your arms extended in front of you. This simple stretch helps release tension in the body, promoting a sense of calm and relaxation by alleviating accumulated tension.

3. **Bridge Pose (Setu Bandhasana):** Lying on your back, slowly raise your hips toward the ceiling, keeping your feet firmly planted on the ground. This pose opens the chest and encourages deep breathing, promoting relaxation and

facilitating the circulation of oxygen and energy through the body.

4. **Downward Facing Dog (Adho Mukha Svanasana):** This inverted pose stimulates blood circulation to the brain, reducing tension in the upper body and promoting a sense of overall well-being by increasing blood flow and improving mental clarity.

Muscle Relaxation and Vagus Nerve Stimulation

The vagus nerve is not only responsible for the body's relaxation response but also plays a crucial role in integrating the body and mind. By stimulating the vagus nerve through techniques such as progressive muscle relaxation and yoga, we are not only improving our physiology, but we are also creating a mental space of serenity and centering.

When the body is relaxed, the mind is free to release confusion and stress. The vagus nerve facilitates communication between the brain and the body, allowing the nervous system to respond more effectively to daily challenges. Every time you practice one of the relaxation exercises described in this chapter, you are not only lowering your stress levels but also training your body to respond more efficiently to stressors and emotional triggers, thereby enhancing your physical and emotional resilience.

Muscle relaxation and yoga are powerful tools to stimulate the vagus nerve and promote overall well-being. By incorporating these techniques into your daily routine, you will not only help reduce stress and improve your quality of life, but you will also discover a new connection between your body and mind—a connection that will allow you to face any challenge with calmness, mindfulness, and inner peace.

Remember: the body and mind are in constant communication. When you learn to relax your body, your mind will follow, and together, you will activate the power of the vagus nerve to restore balance and inner peace.

CHAPTER 9: THE VAGUS NERVE AND EMOTIONAL WELL-BEING

Imagine you're having a particularly stressful day. Your heart is racing, your mind is spinning, and you feel every negative emotion coursing through your body like an electric shock. Now, imagine being able to interrupt this spiral of stress, to stop and quickly find a sense of calm and centeredness. That's what the vagus nerve can offer you: a biological reset for your emotional system. In this chapter, we'll explore how the vagus nerve is key to regulating your emotions and how it can strengthen your emotional resilience, enhancing your ability to face daily challenges.

The vagus nerve is one of the most fascinating and powerful nerves in our bodies. Part of the parasympathetic nervous system, the vagus nerve is responsible for calming the body after it has been activated by the sympathetic nervous system, which triggers the fight-or-flight response. When we activate the vagus nerve, the body and mind prepare to relax and recover from stress, promoting an ideal internal environment for emotional well-being.

Our emotional state is intrinsically linked to our physiology. Emotions are not just something we "feel" in the mind, but are deeply rooted in the body. Fear, anxiety, anger, but also joy, serenity, and love, produce physical changes that can be measured, such as increased heart rate, muscle tension, or shallow breathing. The ability to regulate these physiological responses enables us to manage emotions in a balanced way. And this is where the vagus nerve comes in, our invisible ally that helps us find serenity, even in emotional storms.

The Role of the Vagus Nerve in Regulating Emotions

To understand the role of the vagus nerve in managing emotions, we must first know how its interaction with the brain and body works. The vagus nerve acts as a sort of biological brake that reduces the activity of the sympathetic nervous system, which is activated during stress. When the vagus nerve is active and its tone is high, the body enters a state of relaxation, which in turn promotes more balanced emotions.

When we face stressful situations, our sympathetic nervous system takes over, and our body goes into "fight or flight" mode. The heart accelerates, the muscles contract, and breathing becomes more shallow. This state is useful for dealing with dangerous situations, but if it persists too long, it can lead to physical and emotional discomfort, such as anxiety and depression. The vagus nerve, on the other hand, stimulates the parasympathetic nervous system, which reduces the heart rate, promotes deep breathing, and relaxes the muscles. It is thanks to this activation that we can "brake" the emotional wave, bringing the body and mind back to a state of balance.

This ability to regulate emotions is crucial for our emotional well-being. When the vagal tone is high (the level of activity of the vagus nerve), we are more resilient to daily difficulties. Challenges do not overwhelm us, but we can face them with calm, composure, and clarity. In other words, a strong vagal tone is synonymous with greater emotional resilience.

How to Strengthen Vagal Tone to Improve Emotional Resilience

The good news is that we can improve vagal tone through specific techniques that stimulate the vagus nerve and promote a physiological response of relaxation. In this way, we can train our body and mind to react better to stress, increasing our emotional resilience. The most effective practices include meditation, mindfulness, and physical exercise, which stimulate the vagus nerve and help us maintain a state of emotional well-being.

Meditation and Mindfulness: The Way to Inner Calm

Meditation is one of the most effective practices for stimulating the vagus nerve and improving emotional regulation. Meditation helps slow the heartbeat, reduce muscle tension, and promote awareness of the present moment. When we practice meditation, we can focus on our breathing, listen to our body, and manage our thoughts and emotions. This state of mindfulness promotes the activation of the vagus nerve and reduces emotional reactivity.

A type of meditation that is particularly useful for stimulating the vagus nerve is deep breathing meditation. Every deep, conscious breath we take stimulates the vagus nerve, activating the body's relaxation response. Slow, deep breathing not only reduces immediate stress, but also helps regulate the nervous system in the long term, improving our ability to deal with strong, intense emotions.

Emotional Awareness: Learning to "Feel" Without Being Overwhelmed

Emotional awareness involves paying mindful attention to our emotions, without judgment. Instead of trying to ignore or suppress what we feel, we learn to recognize and accept every emotion that arises in our body. This does not mean being passive or powerless when facing emotions, but rather developing the ability to observe them without being overwhelmed by them. Awareness helps us slow down the emotional response, allowing us to choose how to react in a more balanced way.

When we train ourselves to be aware of emotions without judging them, we stimulate the vagus nerve and promote a parasympathetic response. In practice, we learn not to react impulsively to emotions, but to let them unfold without being overwhelmed.

Physical Exercise: A Silent Ally of the Vagus Nerve

Physical exercise is another powerful way to stimulate the vagus nerve and improve emotional well-being. Regular physical activity reduces levels of cortisol (the stress hormone), promotes the production of endorphins (the feel-good hormones), and improves the function of the autonomic nervous system, including the vagus nerve. In particular, aerobic exercises, such as brisk walking, light jogging, or even dancing, are excellent for stimulating vagal tone.

Physical exercise also helps improve sleep quality, reduce anxiety, and promote a greater sense of psychological well-being. It is a true natural reset for the body and mind, which helps bring the nervous system back into balance.

The vagus nerve is our hidden ally in emotional regulation. Strengthening its tone means not only reducing stress but also boosting our emotional resilience, allowing us to face life with greater serenity and awareness. Meditation, mindfulness, and physical exercise are powerful practices that we can integrate into our daily lives to stimulate the vagus nerve and improve our emotional well-being. Every time you choose to take a moment to breathe deeply, meditate, or move, you are strengthening your vagus nerve and creating an inner state that promotes calm, serenity, and emotional strength. Don't underestimate the power at your disposal: every small gesture you make to stimulate the vagus nerve is a step towards greater internal balance.

CHAPTER 10: THE VAGUS NERVE AND STRESS MANAGEMENT

Imagine a day filled with challenges: a crucial meeting, a pressing deadline, incessant notifications invading your mental space. Your body responds with a racing heart, tense muscles, and a mind in turmoil. You feel like you're under attack, but from what? This reaction is the result of your sympathetic nervous system in action. That's where your best ally comes in: the vagus nerve.

Stress and Its Effect on the Body

To understand the role of the vagus nerve in managing stress, it's important to recognize how stress affects the body. Stress is a primitive physiological response, designed to protect us in emergency situations. However, in the modern world, this response is often triggered by non-threatening stimuli, such as deadlines or everyday worries. This prolonged state of hyperarousal causes an increase in cortisol levels, which can lead to anxiety, insomnia, digestive problems, and other physical ailments.

The vagus nerve, a key component of the parasympathetic nervous system, acts as a "counterbalance" to this response, helping the body return to a balanced state. When activated, it reduces heart rate, relaxes muscles, and lowers stress levels.

Stimulating the Vagus Nerve: Effective Strategies

Here are some effective strategies to activate the vagus nerve and promote a calming response:

1. Neck Massage

A light massage in the neck area, just below the Adam's apple, can directly stimulate the vagus nerve. This area, rich in nerve endings, responds well to a gentle touch, promoting immediate relaxation.

2. Cold Water Immersion

Immersing your face in cold water or taking a

short cold shower activates the vagus nerve. This type of exposure creates an automatic response in the body, reducing stress and promoting deep relaxation.

3. Regular Exercise

Even moderate activity, such as a brisk walk or stretching, helps stimulate the vagus nerve and improve vagal tone. Exercise also helps lower cortisol levels and improve overall mood.

4. Social Interaction

Positive social interactions, such as meaningful conversation or time spent with loved ones, activate the vagus nerve. Connecting with others reduces stress and promotes a sense of well-being.

5. Balanced Diet

A diet rich in fresh, nutrient-dense foods supports the health of the gut microbiota, which is closely linked to the vagus nerve. Including fermented foods or probiotics can further enhance this communication and promote a state of relaxation.

Building a Stress-Relief Routine

Integrating these practices into your day can make a significant difference in your ability to manage stress. Here's an example:

- **Morning:** Start with a few minutes of stretching to wake up your body.
- **During the Day:** Take a break for a brisk walk or a relaxing neck massage.
- **Evening:** End with a cool shower or a chat with a loved one to relax and promote deep sleep.

The vagus nerve is a powerful tool for counteracting the negative effects of stress. With these simple strategies, you can activate it and promote a state of calm and resilience. Every small step toward wellness is an act of self-care. Start today: choose a practice, incorporate it into your routine, and experience the benefits your vagus nerve has to offer.

CHAPTER 11: THE VAGUS NERVE AND SOCIAL CONNECTION

Imagine walking into a room full of people. Without speaking a word, your gaze meets that of another person, and a genuine smile forms naturally. There is an immediate sense of communication, something that goes beyond words, making you feel seen, understood, and accepted. This is the magic of social connection, a bond that is not only formed through words but through an invisible and powerful network that connects us all: our vagus nerve.

In this chapter, we will explore the crucial role of the vagus nerve in building and maintaining our social relationships. We will see how this nerve affects our ability to communicate nonverbally, perceive and respond to physical contact, and how, through vagal tone, it can profoundly improve the quality of our interactions. You will discover how stimulating this nerve can not only enhance your well-being but also strengthen the bond with those around you.

The Vagus Nerve: An Invisible Link

The vagus nerve is the primary communication pathway between the brain and the body, but its influence extends far beyond vital physical functions like heart rate and digestion. It also acts as a social regulator: it directly impacts our ability to connect with others, sense and respond to emotions, and establish meaningful relationships. The key to all of this lies in vagal tone.

What is Vagal Tone?

Vagal tone refers to the ability of the vagus nerve to regulate physiological responses in a way that promotes a balance between stimulation and relaxation. It represents our "readiness" to respond adaptively to social stimuli, especially emotional ones. When vagal tone is high, we are more relaxed, empathetic, and able to perceive emotional cues from others. Low vagal tone, on the other hand, is associated with feelings of isolation and stress.

The good news is that vagal tone can be trained

and improved, leading to more genuine and empathetic social interactions. High vagal tone is linked to greater empathy, smoother communication, and a better ability to interpret nonverbal cues.

The Vagus Nerve and Nonverbal Communication

Much of our social interaction occurs through nonverbal communication: facial expressions, body language, tone of voice, and gestures. The vagus nerve regulates many of these aspects, directly influencing the quality of our interactions. High vagal tone promotes spontaneous smiles, friendly facial expressions, and warm vocal tones, all of which convey empathy and create a sense of safety and connection.

Physical Touch and the Vagus Nerve

Physical touch is a powerful way to stimulate the vagus nerve and promote social connection. Hugs, handshakes, or simple gestures of positive contact can influence our nervous system, inducing feelings of calm and security. This not only strengthens social bonds but also triggers the release of oxytocin, the "feel-good" hormone, which fosters a sense of belonging and connection.

Strategies to Improve Vagal Tone

Here are some daily practices to stimulate the vagus nerve and improve your interpersonal relationships:

1. **Moderate physical activity:** Walking, gentle exercise, or yoga can improve vagal tone, fostering a deeper connection with your body and others.

2. **Active listening:** Paying close attention, without distractions, to the people you are talking to and showing genuine interest is an excellent way to stimulate the vagus nerve and enhance social connection.

3. **Promote physical contact:** Never underestimate the power of a hug or a handshake. These simple gestures can have a significant impact on your well-being and that of those around you.

4. **Cultivate moments of gratitude:** Gratitude can lower stress levels and increase a sense of connection, indirectly improving vagal tone.

Investing in your vagal tone means not only

nurturing your own well-being but also strengthening the bonds that link you to others. With small
daily actions, you can improve your relationships,
creating a sense of intimacy and security that
enriches your life and the lives of those around you.

CHAPTER 12: THE VAGUS NERVE IN MODERN MEDICINE

The human body is an intricate system of electrical and chemical signals, and one of its key components is the vagus nerve. Stretching from the brain to the chest and abdomen, this nerve is more than just a nerve pathway that regulates vital functions like heart rate and digestion. It is our "communication system" between the brain and the body, a conduit that allows our bodies to respond to internal and external stimuli with remarkable precision. But what makes the vagus nerve truly fascinating is its therapeutic potential: not only for our daily well-being, but also for the treatment of a variety of complex conditions. In this chapter, we explore how modern medicine is using technological innovations and advanced devices to stimulate the vagus nerve, opening new doors in the treatment of conditions such as depression, chronic pain, and epilepsy.

Vagal Stimulation: A New Chapter in Medical Therapy

Over the past few decades, medical research has revealed that stimulating the vagus nerve can have extraordinary effects on our mental and physical health. Vagus nerve stimulation has become an innovative therapeutic approach, used to treat a variety of conditions that have traditionally been difficult to manage. But how exactly does vagus nerve stimulation work, and why is it so powerful?

Vagal Stimulation: How Does It Work?

The principle behind vagus nerve stimulation is straightforward, yet extremely effective. The vagus nerve is a cranial nerve that connects the brain to many vital organs, including the heart, lungs, and gut. When stimulated, the vagus nerve sends signals to the brain that regulate and modulate the response of the autonomic nervous system, directly influencing both physical and psychological functions. Vagus nerve stimulation can be delivered via implanted or non-invasive devices, and can have positive effects in terms of reducing stress, improving mood, and even alleviating symptoms of various medical conditions.

Vagal Stimulation in the Treatment of Depression

Depression is one of the most common mental disorders in the world, and traditional treatment is based on antidepressant medications and psychotherapy. However, not all patients respond positively to these therapies, and research has shown that a significant portion of patients do not achieve lasting improvement. This is where vagus nerve stimulation (VNS) comes in, an innovative therapy that has shown promising results, especially in cases of treatment-resistant depression.

In the treatment of depression, a vagus nerve stimulator is surgically implanted under the skin, usually in the chest. This device sends electrical impulses to the vagus nerve, which then stimulates the brain and affects the limbic system, the area of the brain responsible for emotions. Studies have shown that this stimulation can significantly reduce the symptoms of depression, especially in those patients who have not responded to medications.

Clinical studies have demonstrated that vagus nerve stimulation can not only improve mood and reduce anxiety, but also increase resilience to stressful situations. Additionally, vagus nerve stimulation can enhance the effectiveness of antidepressant medications, making it a powerful therapeutic combination for those struggling with chronic depression.

Vagal Stimulation in the Treatment of Chronic Pain

Chronic pain is another debilitating disorder that has traditionally been difficult to treat with conventional methods. It is a condition that can have a devastating impact on quality of life, leading to anxiety, depression, and a general sense of helplessness. Vagus nerve stimulation has been shown to be effective in the treatment of chronic pain, particularly pain associated with conditions such as rheumatoid arthritis, fibromyalgia, and neuropathic pain.

The mechanism behind its effectiveness appears to be the ability of the vagus nerve to modulate the activity of the central nervous system and regulate inflammatory responses. When stimulated, the vagus nerve sends signals to the brain that interfere with pain pathways, reducing the perception of pain and improving quality of life. Some studies suggest that vagus nerve stimulation may also reduce systemic inflammation, a major contributor to many painful conditions.

This approach is particularly appealing to chronic pain sufferers who have not found relief from traditional drug treatments. Vagus nerve stimulation offers an alternative, non-invasive solution that can reduce pain without the side effects associated with medications.

Epilepsy is a neurological disorder that causes recurrent seizures and, in severe cases, can significantly impair the quality of life. Although anticonvulsant drugs are the mainstay of treatment, many patients continue to experience seizures despite medication. Vagus nerve stimulation has been approved as a therapy for drug-resistant epilepsy, with promising results.

In the treatment of epilepsy, vagus nerve stimulation works by influencing the brain circuits involved in seizures. Consistent stimulation of the vagus nerve has been shown to reduce the frequency and severity of seizures, significantly improving the daily lives of patients. Additionally, some studies suggest that vagus nerve stimulation may also improve cognitive function and sleep quality in patients with epilepsy.

Advances in Vagus Nerve Stimulation Technology

Technological advancements in vagus nerve stimulation continue to evolve. Today, there are non-invasive devices available that do not require surgery. These portable devices can be applied directly to the skin, like a patch or bandage, to stimulate the vagus nerve. They are often used for short-term therapeutic purposes, such as mood enhancement or stress management, and are gaining popularity as tools for improving overall well-being.

Another emerging field involves the use of neurofeedback combined with vagus nerve stimulation. This technology allows real-time monitoring and adjustment of brain activity in response to vagal stimulation. These advanced systems are showing promise in treating both psychological and neurological disorders, offering new opportunities for personalized treatment.

The vagus nerve, long recognized as a key link between the body and the brain, is emerging as a natural therapeutic agent capable of profoundly influencing both our physical and mental health. Innovations in vagus nerve stimulation, whether through implanted or non-invasive devices, are opening new possibilities for treating complex conditions such as depression, chronic pain, and epilepsy.

Vagus nerve stimulation is not merely a therapy for chronic diseases. It also represents a more integrated approach to medicine, one that recognizes the fundamental connection between body and mind for our overall well-being. When properly stimulated, the vagus nerve can become a powerful ally in managing stress, alleviating symptoms of various conditions, and improving the quality of life.

The potential of vagus nerve stimulation is still being explored, but the future looks promising. If you are seeking an innovative and scientifically supported approach to improving your well-being, vagus nerve stimulation could be the key to a significant positive change in your life.

CHAPTER 13: THE VAGUS NERVE AND GUT HEALTH

Have you ever experienced stomach discomfort when you're stressed or anxious? Or have you noticed how your digestion slows down under pressure? This is no coincidence. Our gut and brain are closely connected, and this connection is known as the gut-brain axis. The vagus nerve, an often overlooked but incredibly powerful player, plays a crucial role in this communication. In this chapter, we'll explore how this nerve can become a key ally in improving gut health, treating common conditions like irritable bowel syndrome (IBS), and promoting a healthier balance of our gut microbiome.

The Vagus Nerve: A Bridge Between the Brain and the Gut

The vagus nerve is a "superhighway" connecting our brain to numerous vital organs, including the heart, lungs, and, of course, the gut. It is part of the autonomic nervous system and regulates many essential functions, such as heart rate, digestion, and immune response.

This connection between the brain and the gut is not only anatomical but also functional. The vagus nerve is essential for intestinal motility, or the movement of food and waste through the digestive tract, and for regulating the secretion of digestive enzymes. It also modulates inflammatory responses in the gut, thereby influencing the composition of the gut's microbiome, an ecosystem of microorganisms that plays a crucial role in our health.

The Link Between the Vagus Nerve and Irritable Bowel Syndrome

Irritable bowel syndrome (IBS) is one of the most common intestinal disorders, characterized by symptoms such as abdominal pain, bloating, diarrhea, and constipation. Stress and impaired communication between the brain and the gut can trigger these symptoms. This is where the vagus nerve comes into play.

Studies have shown that proper vagus nerve stimulation can relieve IBS symptoms by rebalancing gut motility and reducing inflammation. A healthy vagus nerve acts as a "reset button" for the digestive tract, improving communication between the brain and the gut, and promoting more efficient, less painful digestion.

Vagal Stimulation and the Gut Microbiome

The gut microbiome, comprising trillions of microorganisms, is essential for digestion and has a significant impact on the immune system, metabolism, and even mood. Imbalances in the microbiome can lead to gastrointestinal and systemic disorders.

Vagal stimulation can positively influence the gut microbiome, promoting the growth of beneficial bacterial strains and reducing pathogenic ones. In this way, it helps restore a healthy balance in the gut, reducing inflammation and dysbiosis.

Methods to Stimulate the Vagus Nerve

There are several ways to stimulate the vagus nerve, thus improving gut health:

1. Relaxation Techniques

Practices such as yoga and meditation help activate the parasympathetic nervous system, of which the vagus nerve is a key element. Through specific postures and moments of mental relaxation, these activities can improve intestinal function and promote a balanced microbiome.

2. Exposure to Cold

Exposure to cold temperatures, such as cold showers or immersions in ice water, can activate the vagus nerve, helping to regulate intestinal function and reduce inflammation.

3. Vocal Stimulation

Singing, producing deep sounds, or creating low, vibrating sounds stimulates the vagus nerve through the vocal cords, improving communication between the brain and the gut.

4. Advanced Technologies

Non-invasive vagal nerve stimulation devices, such as patches, are an innovative option to activate the vagus nerve and improve gut health.

Taking care of the vagus nerve is essential not only for intestinal health but also for overall well-being. With natural and modern techniques that can be combined with each other, we can effectively address disorders such as IBS and improve our physical and emotional balance.

CHAPTER 14: THE IMPORTANCE OF SLEEP AND THE VAGUS NERVE

Imagine waking up feeling rested, with a clear mind and an energized body, ready to take on the day. This isn't just a dream—it's a reality you can achieve by improving the quality of your sleep and supporting your nervous system. In particular, the vagus nerve plays a crucial role in promoting deep, restorative sleep.

In an age where insomnia and sleep disorders are increasingly common, understanding how to care for your body to improve sleep quality is essential. During sleep, the body repairs itself, the brain consolidates memories and processes the day's experiences, and the nervous system rebalances.

Sleep: A Vital Process for Recovery

Sleep is not just a break—it's a critical process for recovery. Throughout the night, the body restores energy, repairs tissues, and eliminates accumulated toxins. Research shows that inadequate or poor sleep can lead to negative outcomes such as cardiovascular issues, metabolic imbalances, anxiety, and cognitive difficulties.

The quality of sleep depends on the balance between the sympathetic nervous system, responsible for the 'fight or flight' response, and the parasympathetic system, which promotes relaxation. The vagus nerve, a key component of the parasympathetic system, is crucial for achieving this balance.

The Vagus Nerve and Its Impact on Sleep

The vagus nerve helps the body shift from a state of tension to one of relaxation, creating optimal conditions for deep sleep. When activated, the vagus nerve slows the heart rate, reduces blood pressure, and promotes a sense of calm. This process also helps alleviate obsessive thoughts and mental hyperactivity, which are major causes of insomnia.

Effective Strategies to Stimulate the Vagus Nerve and Enhance Sleep Quality

Here are some practical techniques you can incorporate into your nightly routine to stimulate the vagus nerve and improve sleep:

1. Slow Stretching

Gentle movements and relaxing stretches can help relieve muscle tension and prepare the body for rest. Spend a few minutes doing simple exercises, such as stretching your back or neck, to calm your nervous system.

2. Hot Baths or Showers

Soaking in warm water or taking a relaxing shower before bed can help relax your muscles and reduce the stress accumulated during the day. This habit creates an ideal environment to promote peaceful sleep.

3. Listening to Relaxing Sounds

Soft music, nature sounds, or white noise can create a calming atmosphere, perfect for relaxing the nervous system. You can also try using instruments like tuning forks or other vibrational sounds that stimulate the vagus nerve.

4. Vocal Stimulation Techniques

Humming, singing, or making guttural sounds can directly stimulate the vagus nerve, promoting a state of relaxation. This practice is simple and can be done just before bed.

5. Diet and Evening Rhythms

Avoid heavy or stimulating meals before bed. Include foods rich in magnesium and other nutrients that support the nervous system, such as leafy green vegetables and nuts. A warm cup of herbal tea can complete your evening ritual.

The Vagus Nerve's Role in Combating Insomnia

When stress levels rise, the sympathetic nervous system can remain hyperactive, interfering with sleep. Stimulating the vagus nerve helps to restore balance, reducing cortisol levels and promoting deep, restorative sleep.

Good sleep, supported by a healthy vagus nerve, is the foundation of a balanced life. Integrating some of the strategies described above into your nightly routine will help you experience better rest, waking up with energy and clarity each morning. Choose today to take care of your well-being—your sleep and your vagus nerve will be your most precious allies.

CHAPTER 15: THE VAGUS NERVE AND SPIRITUALITY

Imagine yourself in a state of deep spiritual connection, where your mind is freed from persistent thoughts and your body reaches a sense of peace and well-being. This state is not only a reflection of your physical and mental balance, but it can also represent a gateway to a more profound and authentic spiritual experience. In this chapter, we will explore the profound connection between the vagus nerve and your spiritual journey, and how its stimulation can foster a deeper connection with yourself and the universe, amplifying your inner experience.

Spirituality and the Body: A Deep Connection

Spirituality is often experienced as an inner journey, a path towards a deeper connection with the divine or with a universal force. Whether it is a religious practice, philosophical exploration, or simple introspection, spirituality has the power to transform the perception of yourself and the world around you. It is not only a mental and emotional process: the body plays a fundamental role. Through connection with the body, we stimulate physiological responses that allow us to live deeper experiences. The vagus nerve, a key part of the parasympathetic nervous system, serves as a bridge between body and spirit, allowing us to access states of awareness and inner peace.

What is the Vagus Nerve and Why is it Important for Spirituality?

The vagus nerve is the main component of the parasympathetic nervous system and regulates relaxation and regeneration responses. When stimulated, it promotes a state of calm that reduces stress and helps us achieve balance. From a spiritual perspective, this stimulation can be seen as a "gateway" that allows us to access a deeper connection with ourselves and the divine.

When the vagus nerve is active, mind and body align, promoting reflection, introspection, and greater sensitivity to what surrounds us. Stimulating the vagus nerve not only promotes psychophysical well-being, but it also deepens the spiritual experience, allowing us to perceive our connection with the universe in a more authentic way.

The Vagus Nerve and the Connection with Spirituality

When the vagus nerve is stimulated, the mind opens to new experiences and perceptions. This openness is essential to deepen the spiritual connection and amplify the inner experience. A properly activated vagus nerve allows you to enter a state of deep calm, promoting reflection and awareness, which are essential to experience an authentic spiritual journey. In this state of tranquility, it is easier to perceive the sense of union with the universe and connection with something greater.

Practices to Stimulate the Vagus Nerve and Enhance Spirituality

In addition to the practices already mentioned, there are other activities that can stimulate the vagus nerve and enhance your spiritual experience:

1. Silence and Reflection

Spending time in quiet contemplation, perhaps in a natural environment, promotes the relaxation of the nervous system and stimulates awareness, creating space for spiritual connection.

2. Relaxing or Sacred Music

Listening to soothing melodies, sacred chants, or nature sounds can activate the vagus nerve and bring you to a state of tranquility and openness.

3. Conscious Movement

Practices such as yoga or tai chi integrate movement and breathing, stimulating the vagus nerve and creating a state of balance between body and mind.

4. Connecting with Nature

Spending time outdoors, walking barefoot on the grass, or simply watching a sunset can have a powerful calming effect on the nervous system and amplify your connection with the universe.

Stimulating the vagus nerve is not only a means of improving physical and mental well-being, but also a way to deepen your spiritual experience. Through practices that integrate body, mind, and spirit, you can discover new dimensions of awareness and inner peace, and cultivate a deeper connection with yourself and the universe.

CHAPTER 16: THE VAGUS NERVE IN PERFORMANCE IMPROVEMENT

When we think about performance, whether cognitive, physical, or professional, we often focus on effort, determination, and strategies. However, there is one crucial element often overlooked: our nervous system. In particular, the vagus nerve plays a vital role in managing stress, aiding recovery from fatigue, and optimizing performance, ranging from physical activity to mental focus. In this chapter, we explore how vagus nerve stimulation can positively influence your abilities, offering practical techniques to enhance focus, mental endurance, and recovery.

The Vagus Nerve and Performance: A Subtle but Powerful Connection

The vagus nerve, a key component of the

parasympathetic nervous system, is known for its role in regulating the body's physiological responses. When the vagus nerve is active, we are better able to cope with stress and recover quickly. This natural response not only helps us stay calm and clear during high-pressure situations, but also improves our ability to focus and maintain high physical and mental performance.

Concentration: The Vagus Nerve as a Gateway

Concentration is a vital component of performance. However, in modern life, distractions and stress often hinder our ability to focus. When we stimulate the vagus nerve, the parasympathetic nervous system activates, promoting a state of calm that facilitates greater mental clarity. This allows us to reduce distractions and focus on important tasks, increasing productivity and performance.

An easy way to improve concentration is to integrate activities into your routine that relax the nervous system, such as listening to calming music or using positive visualization techniques.

Mental Toughness: Pushing Beyond the Limits

Mental toughness is the ability to persevere in

the face of challenges and difficulties. Thanks to its role as a regulator of the nervous system, the vagus nerve helps us remain calm under pressure and overcome critical moments. This response reduces the impact of psychological stress, allowing you to face difficulties with greater strength and clarity.

Techniques such as vagus nerve massage or the adoption of relaxing practices during work breaks can help increase mental resilience and maintain a high level of performance even in difficult conditions.

Recovery: Return to Balance

Recovery is essential to maintain high performance over time. After each effort, the vagus nerve helps the body and mind return to a state of balance, facilitating restorative processes. This ability to recover is not only about physical regeneration, but also about restoring mental clarity and motivation.

Integrating practices such as stretching, massage, or listening to relaxing music into your routine can speed up recovery, reduce the perception of fatigue, and optimize your general well-being.

Practical Techniques to Stimulate the Vagus Nerve and Improve Performance

Here are some practical techniques you can implement in your daily life to optimize concentration, mental endurance, and recovery:

1. Vagus Nerve Massage

Gently massaging the area behind the ears or along the neck can stimulate the vagus nerve, reducing stress and improving recovery.

2. Positive Visualization Techniques

Imagining positive and motivating scenarios can activate the parasympathetic nervous system, helping you stay calm and focused.

3. Gentle Stretching

Practicing gentle stretching not only reduces muscle tension, but also stimulates the parasympathetic nervous system, improving recovery.

4. Listening to Relaxing Music

Calming music is a powerful stimulus for the vagus nerve, promoting relaxation and better stress management.

The vagus nerve is not only a component of the nervous system, but also a valuable ally in improving performance. Stimulating it regularly will help you develop greater concentration, superior mental endurance, and faster recovery. Integrating these techniques into your daily routine will allow you to successfully face life's challenges and excel in every area, from work to sports.

CHAPTER 17: VAGUS NERVE AND LONGEVITY

Imagine your body as a finely tuned system, designed to function efficiently over time without overheating, maintaining its power and vitality year after year. This system is our body, and one of the most crucial and often overlooked elements that contribute to its optimal functioning is the vagus nerve. Recent research has shown that vagal tone—the activity and efficiency of the vagus nerve—is a key indicator of a long, healthy life.

In this chapter, we will explore how the vagus nerve impacts our daily well-being and how it plays a critical role in preventing chronic diseases, helping to maintain health and longevity. We will discover that taking care of the vagus nerve is a fundamental step in enhancing life quality and ensuring long-lasting wellness.

Vagal Tone: An Indicator of Health and Longevity

To understand how the vagus nerve can influence longevity, it's important to first understand the concept of "vagal tone." This term refers to the level of activity of the vagus nerve and its ability to balance the sympathetic nervous system (which responds to danger by triggering the "fight or flight" response) and the parasympathetic system (which promotes relaxation and recovery).

A high vagal tone indicates that the body can effectively respond to external stimuli and recover quickly from stress, while a low vagal tone is often linked to greater susceptibility to chronic diseases. Maintaining good vagal tone is therefore essential for keeping the body in balance and preventing numerous health problems.

The Vagus Nerve and the Immune System

The vagus nerve not only regulates the nervous system but also plays a key role in modulating the immune system. It does so through the "vagal reflex," which helps reduce inflammation in the body. Chronic inflammation is a risk factor for many diseases, including cardiovascular diseases, diabetes, and certain types of cancer. Stimulating the vagus nerve can help reduce inflammation, protect the body, and promote a healthy, long life.

Vagus Nerve, Stress, and Chronic Disease

The vagus nerve is vital in managing stress, a major risk factor for long-term health. An active vagus nerve allows the body to quickly restore balance after experiencing stress. However, low vagal tone diminishes this ability, increasing the risk of developing conditions such as:

- **Cardiovascular diseases**: Chronic stress raises blood pressure and heart rate. A healthy vagus nerve helps keep these parameters in check.
- **Metabolic disorders**: Low vagal tone is linked to obesity and type 2 diabetes, as the vagus nerve helps regulate metabolism.
- **Neurodegenerative diseases**: Stress and chronic inflammation are risk factors for conditions like Alzheimer's and Parkinson's disease. Good vagal tone helps protect the brain.

Techniques to Stimulate the Vagus Nerve and Support Longevity

There are several daily practices that you can integrate into your routine to stimulate the vagus nerve and improve overall health, thus contributing to longevity:

1. **Regular physical activity**: Moderate aerobic exercise, such as walking, swimming, or jogging, stimulates the vagus nerve, helping to reduce stress and improve cardiovascular health.
2. **Relaxation techniques**: Practices such as yoga and Tai Chi, which combine movement and mindfulness, are particularly effective in strengthening vagal tone and promoting deep relaxation.
3. **Exposure to cold**: Cold showers or baths activate the vagus nerve, improving stress resilience and stimulating the immune system.
4. **Sound stimulation**: Harmonic sounds, such as nature sounds or calming melodies, can activate the vagus nerve,

reducing inflammation and improving
both mental and physical well-being.

Taking care of the vagus nerve means taking care of your long-term health. By incorporating these simple practices into your daily life, you will enhance your quality of life, prevent chronic diseases, and enjoy greater vitality. A healthy vagus nerve is a key ally in living a long, balanced, and energetic life.

CHAPTER 18: INCORPORATING THE VAGUS NERVE INTO YOUR DAILY LIFE

Imagine having a secret ally always by your side, ready to step in when stress becomes overwhelming or fatigue builds up. That ally is your vagus nerve. When properly stimulated, it can become a daily tool for improving your health, energy, and well-being, promoting a balance between your body and mind.

Incorporating vagal stimulation into your daily life may seem like a challenge, but it is actually straightforward and natural. In this chapter, we will explore practical techniques that are easy to include in your routine without complications. The vagus nerve can be activated effortlessly throughout your daily activities, helping you find calm and focus while working, socializing, or relaxing.

The Central Role of the Vagus Nerve

The vagus nerve is the "conductor" of the autonomic nervous system, responsible for essential functions such as your heart rate, digestion, and stress response. When its tone is high, the body manages stress better and recovers quickly from stressful moments. In contrast, a low tone can lead to problems such as anxiety, chronic fatigue, and difficulty relaxing.

Becoming aware of these mechanisms is the first step in integrating the vagus nerve into your daily life. With simple measures, you can improve vagal tone and experience improvements in your physical, mental, and relational health.

1. Self-Care Practices: Slow Down and Recover

Modern life encourages us to constantly rush, but the vagus nerve thrives when we take moments to slow down and recover. It's not about turning your day upside down, but about integrating small restorative breaks:

- **Mindful lunch break:** Eating at a slow pace and mindfully reduces stress and promotes digestion. Spend 15 minutes on your meal, savoring each bite without distractions.

- **Relaxing activities:** At the end of the day, techniques such as a neck massage, a warm shower, or the use of a weighted blanket can release muscle tension and promote recovery.

2. Movement and Physical Activity

Regular physical activity is a powerful stimulator of the vagus nerve. You don't need to engage in intense workouts: even a daily 20-30 minute walk outside can improve vagal tone, promote digestion, and reduce stress.

Practices like Tai Chi, yoga, and swimming are particularly effective, as they involve slow, deliberate movements and foster body awareness. If you're pressed for time, even a short stretching session can make a difference.

3. Foster Social Connections

Positive social interactions have a profound effect on the vagus nerve. Feeling connected, laughing, and sharing meaningful moments lower stress levels and promote mental well-being.

Make time for social connections every day, even with just a quick phone call, a walk with a friend, or a sincere conversation with a colleague. These moments strengthen emotional bonds and stimulate the parasympathetic system.

4. Optimize Rest and Sleep

Quality sleep is essential for a well-functioning vagus nerve. During the night, the parasympathetic system works to regenerate the body and mind. To improve the quality of sleep:

- **Create a relaxing evening routine**: Turn off electronic devices at least 30 minutes before bed and opt for calming activities, such as reading or listening to relaxing music.
- **Maintain regular hours**: Sleeping and waking up at the same time promotes a stable circadian rhythm and optimal recovery.

Experiment and Listen to Your Body

Incorporating vagus nerve stimulation into your life does not require great effort, but rather small daily adjustments. Every step you take towards improving your vagal tone is an investment in a more balanced, healthy, and happy life.

Try these techniques, observe the changes, and find what works best for you. With your vagus nerve as an ally, wellness becomes an accessible reality every day.

CONCLUSION: THE JOURNEY TO WELLNESS WITH THE VAGUS NERVE

We have begun a fascinating exploration of the connection between the vagus nerve and our physical and mental well-being. We've discovered how this often overlooked and underestimated nerve plays a crucial role in maintaining our mental and physical balance. Now, after examining vagal stimulation techniques and how to incorporate them into daily life, we have reached the end of this chapter, but not the end of our journey.

Vagus nerve stimulation is not a quick fix. It is a profound and lasting change, a practice that needs to be cultivated every day, accompanying you through every stage of your life. Its ability to reduce stress, improve emotional regulation, promote calm, and enhance overall health is not just a theoretical promise—it is a well-established scientific fact. With the vagus nerve as your ally, you can activate your parasympathetic system, the part of your nervous system that helps you calm down, reduce inflammation, and promote both physical and mental recovery.

A Body and Mind in Harmony

We've discussed how daily practices like deep breathing, exercise, social interaction, relaxation, and sleep are essential for activating the vagus nerve. But you might be wondering, "Why is it so important to incorporate these practices into every aspect of my life?" The answer is simple: integrating the vagus nerve into your daily routine helps you lead a more balanced, resilient, and healthy life.

Regular stimulation of the vagus nerve helps you build a healthier stress response. It not only improves your ability to handle life's challenges but also allows you to recover more quickly, boost your energy, and enjoy long-lasting well-being. Essentially, the vagus nerve is your ally in moments of difficulty or fatigue. Whether you're facing a tough day, involved in an argument, or feeling overwhelmed, you can activate the techniques you've learned to restore balance to your body and mind.

And it's not just a temporary "state of calm."

Vagus nerve stimulation is a process that, if practiced consistently, will transform you. It can help dismantle the barriers that prevent us from living fully, reduce anxiety, and elevate mood, thereby enhancing your overall quality of life. It is an invitation to live more consciously, to slow down, to feel, and to breathe. Every small action, such as taking a deep breath or pausing for a moment during the day, is a step toward integrated well-being.

The Power of Awareness

One of the most powerful aspects of the journey toward wellness through vagus nerve stimulation is the power of awareness. Being mindful of how your body reacts to stress, how emotions influence your physical state, and how you respond to these cues, allows you to be more present and make better decisions for your well-being. Awareness is the key that enables you to transform your daily experience, allowing you to actively choose your internal state instead of reacting passively to external events.

Every step you take toward vagus nerve stimulation is a conscious decision to love yourself, to value your body and mind. It's not a battle to win but a process of healing and listening. The more you learn to care for yourself, the more positively your body will respond, and the more your life will improve.

A Call to Action: Continue Your Journey

Now that you have a deeper understanding of the vagus nerve and how to stimulate it, it's time to take action. Don't let this knowledge remain just theory. Apply what you've learned. Every day presents a new opportunity to improve your well-being, a chance to consciously integrate the vagus nerve into your routine. You don't need to make drastic changes all at once—start with small steps: a deep-breathing break, a walk outside, a few minutes of relaxation before bed. All of these moments will help strengthen your nervous system and improve your overall well-being.

Remember, the journey is never over. Every day, you can do something new, deepen your awareness, and continue to explore the potential of the vagus nerve as a tool for a healthier, balanced, and happier life.

I encourage you to continue with curiosity and dedication. Each step you take will bring you closer to the well-being you deserve, both physically and mentally. Your health is an ongoing journey, and vagus nerve stimulation is a powerful tool to approach it with calm, energy, and strength.

Your New Life Starts Now

Are you ready to begin? Every breath, every mindful moment, every gesture of self-care is a declaration of love towards your body and mind. It is an empowering act, a means of reconnecting with your true self. The vagus nerve is a gateway that opens the door to a more balanced, healthier, and happier life. There's no time like the present—start today.